TOOLS FOR TEACHERS

- **ATOS:** 0.7
- **GRL:** C
- **LEXILE:** 220L
- **CURRICULUM CONNECTIONS:** community helpers, transportation
- **WORD COUNT:** 92

Skills to Teach

- **HIGH-FREQUENCY WORDS:** a, am, an, I, me, the, there, to, us, who
- **CONTENT WORDS:** airplane, bus, captain, city, driver, engineer, ferry, pilot, school, streetcar, train
- **PUNCTUATION:** periods, question marks, apostrophe, exclamation point
- **WORD STUDY:** /s/, spelled c (*city*); /k/, spelled *ch* (*school*); long /i/, spelled *is* (*island*); schwa /ə/, spelled *ai* (*captain*); compound words (*airplane, grandma's, streetcar*); long /e/, spelled *eo* (*people*); r-controlled vowels (*driver, park, store, streetcar*)
- **TEXT TYPE:** information report

Before Reading Activities

- Read the title and give a simple statement of the main idea.
- Have students "walk" though the book and talk about what they see in the pictures.
- Introduce new vocabulary by having students predict the first letter and locate the word in the text.
- Discuss any unfamiliar concepts that are in the text.

After Reading Activities

Encourage children to talk about methods of transportation in the book. Which have they used before, and where did they go? Do they know anyone who drives a school bus, flies a plane, captains a ferry, etc.?

Tadpole Books are published by Jump!, 5357 Penn Avenue South, Minneapolis, MN 55419, www.jumplibrary.com

Copyright ©2018 Jump. International copyright reserved in all countries. No part of this book may be reproduced in any form without written permission from the publisher.

Editor: Jenny Fretland VanVoorst **Designer:** Anna Peterson

Photo Credits: Alamy: Jim West, 5; Felix Choo, 6–7; Ian Lishman, 8; ColorBlind Images, 14–15. Getty: Gregory Herringer/EyeEm, 12. Shutterstock: Vibrant Image Studio, cover; LuckyImages, 1; rasika108, 2–3; Flashon Studio, 3; Cynthia Farmer, 4; Lars Christensen, 8, 14; Sean Hsu, 10; Sam D Cruz, 11; JamesChen, 12; Imfoto, 13; pyzata, 14–15. SuperStock: Digital Vision/Exactostock-1598, 9.

Library of Congress Cataloging-in-Publication Data is available at www.loc.gov or upon request from the publisher.
ISBN: 978-1-62031-763-1 (hardcover)
ISBN: 978-1-62031-783-9 (paperback)
ISBN: 978-1-62496-610-1 (ebook)

WHO HELPS US GET AROUND?

by Erica Donner

TABLE OF CONTENTS

tadpole
books

WHO HELPS US GET AROUND?

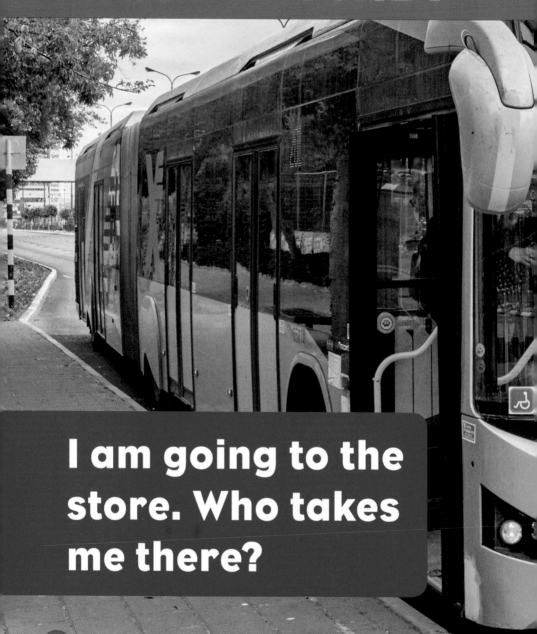

I am going to the store. Who takes me there?

city bus driver

A city bus driver.

I am going to school.
Who takes me there?

A school bus driver.

I am going to the park. Who takes me there?

A streetcar driver.

I am going to
grandma's house.
Who takes me there?

An airplane pilot.

train

I am going to the coast. Who takes me there?

A train engineer.

ferry

I am going to the island. Who takes me there?

A ferry captain.

Who helps us get around?

Lots of people!

WORDS TO KNOW

airplane

city bus

ferry

school bus

streetcar

train

INDEX